CHLOROPHYLL

POETRY

Lunafly
once upon a twin
Bokeh Focus
A Babble of Objects
The Kiss of Walt Whitman Still on My Lips
How to Kill Poetry
Road Work Ahead
Mute
This Way to the Acorns
St. Michael's Fall

FICTION

Widower, 48, Seeks Husband
Compassion, Michigan
Flannelwood
The Last Deaf Club in America
The Kinda Fella I Am
Men with Their Hands

NONFICTION

A Quiet Foghorn: More Notes from a Deaf Gay Life
From Heart into Art: Interviews with Deaf and Hard of Hearing Artists and Their Allies
Notes of a Deaf Gay Writer: 20 Years Later
Assembly Required: Notes from a Deaf Gay Life
Silence is a Four-Letter Word: On Art & Deafness

DRAMA

Whispers of a Savage Sort and Other Plays about the Deaf American Experience
Snooty: A Comedy

AS EDITOR

Lovejets: Queer Male Poets on 200 Years of Walt Whitman
QDA: A Queer Disability Anthology
Among the Leaves: Queer Male Poets on the Midwestern Experience
Eyes of Desire 2: A Deaf GLBT Reader
When I am Dead: The Writings of George M. Teegarden
Eyes of Desire: A Deaf Gay & Lesbian Reader

Advance Praise for
CHLOROPHYLL

In Raymond Luczak's *Chlorophyll*, the devastating natural beauty of Michigan's Upper Peninsula is imbued with passions its reticent human inhabitants are loathe to express. Trees, lakes, and stones air their infatuations, their grudges, their mythologies and griefs. Through this forest of the otherwise unsaid, we catch glimpses of a speaker who knows there is no line to blur between 'person' and 'nature.' "At sixteen, I found myself in the arms / of a handsome tree," he says, though his could just as well be the voice of basalt calling out from the shores of Lake Superior, "cradle us for a few moments / in the sun, if you don't mind, please."

—Emily Van Kley,
author of *Arrhythmia* and *The Cold and the Rust*

Raymond Luczak conjures the Upper Peninsula of Michigan in poems that weave "together a hint of fire and chlorophyll" and that personify the landscape—a basalt pebble, a birch stand, the brutal cold of winter, the cliffs of Lake Superior. In this rich "tapestry of history," Luczak animates his origin stories amid tree-named streets, eight siblings, and the copper, iron ore, and ghosts of the land. In *Chlorophyll*, Raymond Luczak harnesses the sunlight essential for growth, deftly interlacing words like "fingers enmeshed in prayer against rain."

—Stephanie Heit,
author of *Psych Murders* and *The Color She Gave Gravity*

Raymond Luczak's *Chlorophyll* is a wonder to behold. He invokes the trees, rocks, and shorelines of Michigan's upper peninsula, infusing its topography with legend and lore, love and loss, and the myths of dreams, citing nature's often brutal beauty. The images in these poems are indelible, powerful revelations of both a finite location and the interior world of the poet's imagination, both intimately observed. I will return to these poems again and again, just as the waves of Lake Superior lap against basalt, agate, jaspilite, quartz, and memory.

—Pia Taavila-Borsheim, Ph.D.,
author of *Moon on the Meadow* and *Above the Birch Line*

The poems of *Chlorophyll* have the quality of rich soil. In these origin tales of an animate world, identities are porous. Lava, tears, and ghosts synthesize to create the specific landscape of Michigan's Upper Peninsula, northern cultivated gardens, and interior conservatories. Although love changes to loss, loss composts into visions when "everything will be refitted whole."

—Su Smallen Love,
author of *Kinds of Snow* and *The Memoir of Mona Lisa*

In these beautiful poems, Raymond Luczak translates his youth through the lens of the landscape of Michigan's Upper Peninsula. Giving voice to the natural world, he allows the rocks, trees, lakes, insects, and flowers that are part of flora and fauna of the region to speak for themselves, and they remind us that we are human, living in a more than human world. These poems ache with love for a place left, but never forgotten.

—William Reichard,
author of *Our Delicate Barricades Downed* and
The Night Horse: New and Selected Poems

In *Chlorophyll,* Raymond Luczak takes on a specific region and the ghosts which inhabit it. He does this artfully and in a multi-faceted way by examining the fauna, the geology, the mythology, and the people of upper Michigan. And it is the people who center this fine collection. Luczak speaks to those "already longing / for something real, perhaps / a song."

—Mike James,
author of *Leftover Distances* and *Crows in the Jukebox*

CHLOROPHYLL

poems about michigan's upper peninsula

RAYMOND LUCZAK

MODERN HISTORY PRESS
Ann Arbor, Michigan

Copyright

Chlorophyll: Poems about Michigan's Upper Peninsula
© Copyright 2022 by Raymond Luczak

978-1-61599-642-1 paperback
978-1-61599-643-8 hardcover
978-1-61599-644-5 eBook

Cover Design: Mona Z. Kraculdy
Cover Photograph ("Furnace Lake"): Shawn Malone, Lake Superior Photo (lakesuperiorphoto.com)
Author Photograph: Raymond Luczak

Modern History Press
5145 Pontiac Trail
Ann Arbor, MI 48105
Toll-free: 888-761-6268
Fax: 734-663-6861
E-mail: info@modernhistorypress.com
Web: modernhistorypress.com

Distributed by Ingram (USA/CAN/AU) and Bertram's Books (UK/EU).

Library of Congress Cataloging-in-Publication Data

Names: Luczak, Raymond, 1965- author.
Title: Chlorophyll : poems about Michigan's Upper Peninsula / Raymond
   Luczak.
Description: Ann Arbor, Michigan : Modern History Press, [2022] | Summary:
   "With this poetry collection, the author celebrates the wilderness of
   Michigan's Upper Peninsula. The book's 52 poems not only explore the
   changes of each season but also the inner lives of flora and trees and
   waves alongside Lake Superior"-- Provided by publisher.
Identifiers: LCCN 2022000954 (print) | LCCN 2022000955 (ebook) | ISBN
   9781615996438 (hardcover) | ISBN 9781615996421 (paperback) | ISBN
   9781615996445 (epub)
Subjects: LCSH: Upper Peninsula (Mich.)--Poetry. | LCGFT: Poetry.
Classification: LCC PS3562.U2554 C48 2022 (print) | LCC PS3562.U2554
   (ebook) | DDC 811/.54--dc23/eng/20220112
LC record available at https://lccn.loc.gov/2022000954
LC ebook record available at https://lccn.loc.gov/2022000955

CONTENTS

III

IV

for

Eric Norris

AMYGDALOID

1.

Millions of years ago this was a land of volcanoes.
Lava spewed like lunch. Once the raging cooled off,
everything fell into fissures. Bubbles of oxygen
drowned, trapped into stones of no distinction.

2.

The word "amygdaloid" stems from the Latin word
for "almond." Centuries have smelted it with meanings.
The "amygdalae" stimulates the brain's hypothalamus
into thinking emotion and feeling memory.

3.

In the clearing of woods near the abandoned mines,
the rust of iron is a powder that can't be showered away
even in the luminous rains of April. It's always there,
lurking like the snake of autumn waiting to bite.

4.

The word also refers to the texture of stone
lined with empty hisses. Such stones had to have existed
when the first man and woman discovered the snake
of knowledge in the virgin act of fornication.

5.

Tons of rocks aggregate amidst the merciless torture
the waves of Lake Superior administer nonstop.
The water is a lava-burned woman hell-bent on revenge.
No one will ever breathe again. They must drown.

6.

Agates, far smaller than almonds, grasp at the anchor
of others their kind clinging to the soil underneath
at the edge of the world between water and land.
They dream of never having to time their breaths.

7.

The word is also the name of my high school yearbook.
The brain is a stone filled with lonely vesicles.
Come pour the water of memory into the gaping holes
of what I should remember. I'm far from home.

IMMIGRANTS

Winds from the south flung me, a raindrop, north
where I approached the top tier of the Bond Falls.

Before I parachuted down, I took sight
of the Ontonagon River below me.

Trees stood high like jagged daggers
stuck upside down in the riverbanks.

I prayed the winds would sway me away,
but the pitter-patter below was much too loud.

I crashed right next to a clump of torn grass
off the river. I bounced on a branch of blade and clung.

But my fluid arms and hands grew cold and tired.
I fell asleep into the cascading waters.

Jolted alive, I felt a million arms of strangers
grabbing me as we surged north as one.

The river's width and drops in elevation
only made us tenacious. We were an army of one.

We marched right through the Agate Falls.
We burbled hopes of a Promised Sea.

Out in the mouth of Ontonagon River
onto Lake Superior, stories and legends swirled.

Who knew that we had so much history?
Even the smallest drop has a story.

THE BIRTH OF AGATES

Ghosts dress in only gray and white.
This is how they camouflage their volcanic selves.
Lake Superior is bottled with them.
You can't see them but they move like fish.
They streak lightnings of iced lava.
Their whispers startle walleye and lake sturgeon.
They lurk in the shadow of fishing boats.
Their folds flit around the swaying bait.
They dream of toying with the line.
Laughter from above ripples like thunder.
Their eyes turn dull as yellow perch.
They shed tears of crimson rainbows.
It hurts to wipe away these unfulfilled dreams.
The shores of Lake Superior bloom in agate.

ON DOCKS OFF EAGLE HARBOR

In the east, the moon rises
a contained ball of flame.

Winds surf the anxious waves
and around the lonely docks.

Unfamiliar stars tip their toes
in the vast lake of night.

Stale clouds coat the lighthouse
blinking its tired pulse.

The moon arches even higher
on the ladder with each minute.

The north leaks a faint light,
an unsettling of ghosts long past.

Isle Royale is a shadow,
trees unshaven in the swath.

Sprinkles of water thunder
across the stiffened benches.

Shedding its residue, the moon
sails clean-white on high.

HOW COPPER CAME TO
THE KEWEENAW PENINSULA

A long time ago Venus paid the Keweenaw Peninsula
a visit. She stepped off her gold-encrusted chariot
on the shore off Eagle Harbor. Her horses,
shimmering with the flaxen sun, nibbled
at the wild plants that lined Lake Superior.

Indeed on this beautiful summer day, made
for galloping above the lilting waves, she rested.
She much needed a vacation alone from the chaos
after the Romans forced her half-sister Aphrodite
into exile. She was tired of being watched.

She gathered a bevy of raspberries and strawberries.
Her skin glowed with the flush of fresh blood.
Her toes nestled among agates that nuzzled.
She sat facing the western sun from a fallen log,
worn smooth as sandal against marble.

Up north the darkening skies spewed hues of color.
Her cousin Sagittarius galloped and shot arrows at stars,
not knowing that she was watching, let alone missing.
Her horses settled down to sleep on the sand
next to her. The night air was her blanket.

After so many nights alone in bed, she'd thought
her husband Vulcan would never notice
the emptiness in their bed, or how she'd drifted
into loneliness as she saw how he banished
the rest of the Greek side of her family.

She suddenly heard a distant rumble of hooves
thundering from the east. She squinted at
the chariot silhouette of Vulcan whipping
his horses harder, faster, *now*. Her heart sank
when her horses didn't stop neighing fear.

As he stepped off his chariot, he didn't say
a word. His coal eyes shone the language of fire.
His shoulders were always smoking volcanoes.
He never drank water except to cool off and make love.
His thrusts blurred the line between passion and rage.

His skin, already limning yellow-orange,
was lined with the sweat beads of anger.
He vomited streams of lava bile at her.
But the first volley missed, landing near
Minnesota and Ontario, where it became Isle Royale.

His next expulsion melted down her chariot.
That second flowing just couldn't stop sizzling
everything south of Eagle Harbor except for her,
already floating on the clouds of steam,
weeping at what a stupid concubine she'd become.

He never let her out of his sight until she died.
Centuries later his lava bile became the richest copper,
the very metal that sparked alchemical explorations.
But one alloy after another never turned into gold.
He didn't care. He had drunk himself to death.

JASPILITES

No one remembers how their arguments started.
Zeus said, Hera said—that sort of thing.
It always ended with him aiming thunderbolt arrows
at her. He was a great hunter, but he always missed.
Deliberately. They swore to condemn each other
to the hissing pits of Tartarus, bubbling lava
with not a droplet of water in sight.

Then the Romans came and conquered everything.
Centuries wore down mortals into disbelieving.
Gods and goddesses who roamed the Pantheon were
neutered. But Zeus wasn't ready to retire. Oh, no!
He still taunted Hera with a longer list of her friends
he'd managed to seduce after their first year
of marriage. She pummeled him with pomegranates.

He stood his ground and stared into her eyes.
This time he didn't miss. She stumbled dead
into his arms. They melted in the fire of his tears.
We jaspilites are remainders of their veins.
If you ever find us off the Keweenaw Peninsula,
treasure our remains. One day you too will
bleed thunderbolts and pomegranates.

OFF THE CLIFFS OF LAKE SUPERIOR

The skin
of these walls
are dimpled
with acne

that never clear
after centuries
of moisturizing
rains and snow.

The prickly hairs
of pine trees
make them cringe
and cry in resin.

Only in shadows
do we see
what teenagers
they still are,

hiding secrets
for fear of
being mocked
in sunlight.

BASALT

We are the couch potatoes of rocks.
We just sit there and pray someone notices.
The waves always ignore us.

We are everywhere but nowhere
as exciting—flat, round, and small—
in shades of dark grays and dull browns.

We don't glitter gasps of quartz,
show off our striped lapels and hues,
or gleam spectacular patterns of color.

We're just little guys who's never had
someone tell us how worthy we are.
Agates and amethysts get all the attention.

We're always too afraid to ask for a caress.
We keep dreams of darting among your feet
to ourselves. We often ask why we exist.

If you ever walk near Black River Harbor,
please cradle us for a few moments
in the sun. If you don't mind, please.

WHY GIANTS DON'T EXIST
IN THE UPPER PENINSULA

A long time ago all this was very true.

Giants never rested here in the Porcupine Mountains,
mere inclines lined with trees existing only
for their idle amusement, toughened
as they chased each other, trampling pines
into mere shrubbery. They pealed laughs
louder than church bells clanging
throughout the land. Every single animal
fled in fear of their deathly footprints.
Then came the mating season of fee-*fa*-foo-*fum*s,
the raw trills meant to deafen as the grounds
quaked violently from their consummations.
There was not a tree standing upright left.
Out of boredom, they up and left for the north,
plodding through the puddle of Lake Superior.
These giants had been so long used to being the tallest
of all they'd ever seen, they'd never realized
the depths of death they could sink to
until it was too late. The chill froze their blood,
icing their last thoughts of that magical summer,
wild and crazy up in those tree-carpeted hills.
From the deep they're still gasping for help,
grabbing at anything that floats above them.

That much is still true.

GICHIGAMI
after Lake Superior

1.

My average body temperature is below 36 Fahrenheit.
But I wasn't always that way. It's more efficient to freeze
these men and women as they drown into my arms.

2.

My body is filled with legends and shipwrecks. Open
any one of my 200 tributary veins to siphon blame. Nothing.
The less I surrender, the more dead children I get to keep.

3.

Henry Wadsworth Longfellow called me "Gitche Gumee"
in his turgid book poem *The Song of Hiawatha*. French explorers
called me *le lac supérieur*, the "Upper Lake." Frankly, I never cared.

4.

Researchers have calculated how long I will retain
my secrets before my water's completely changed: 191 years.
So many generations of them, and I'm still the same.

5.

The Ojibwe called me "Gichigami," as in "big water."
It's the only name I like. They were the first to die in my arms.
When they began paying homages to me, I knew I had to kill more.

6.

Fish murmur deep in my stomach. They remind me
how I used to be embraced before the Ice Ages came
to take away my only child. I was never the same again.

7.

When ships and yachts and boats slide across my body,
they turn into the most horrible itches I ache to relieve.
But I hold still my temper. They're still too young to understand.

8.

Everyone says that I am a great big mystery.
I chortle. I am nothing but water that can freeze
humans like they freeze fish they've just caught.

9.

Shipwrecks are the greatest gift I can ever ask for.
I am always careful to time my disturbances when I get
too lonely. Never underestimate a mother's need.

10.

Climate change has begun to give me fevers
I'd never had before. I can't be so mad to let go
of my secrets. Please stop taking my temperature.

11.

I will never give up my dead babies.
I cradle them all in my chilly arms and coo lullabies.
I will never turn out the nightlight.

FOG OFF LITTLE GIRL'S POINT

The air dances
cool kisses
up and down
my spine.

Silence,
such music.

Come wrap me
in your shroud
unrolling
around my feet.

No one knows
I'm still a child.

A GHOST, HALFWAY THERE

She will have died long before her body does.
Words once so easy to use will have failed.
Loss is the most difficult language to master.
It's been years since she's looked into a mirror.
Lake Superior is not for narcissists.

The empty shell of her ribcage drums out
the lost heartbeat never matching her dreams.
Her song has been raked deep from the earth.
Even the dark waters cannot silence the littered
skeletons and shipwrecks laced with kelp.

As she faces the waves whipping up in a fury,
the winds command her to brace against the snap
of ice trying to bend the hairline fractures
tattooed like veins uprooted all over her bones.
No matter how stiffly she stands, she will not break.

ONTONAGON

Deep in the moss of Ontonagon River
are majestic trees felled and bones of bears
hunted, skinned, and roasted with their fat
dripping into the fingers of fire hungry for more
as these hunters, long before the white man,
glanced up at the crisp constellations,
reminding them of yet another tale
about the Great Spirits who roamed the land.
Mornings they left behind shards of bowls
that voluminous snow and silt of spring
would bury, cradling the maws of moose
and lining these magnificent bones
in unmade beds of minuscule copper ore.
One day everything will be refitted whole.

II

THE ORANGE-HAIRED GIRL

Everyone keeps saying how beautiful Autumn looks
even though she's still struggling to smile in her bed.
After one false alarm of death after another,
the doctors keep changing her prognosis.
They marvel at the colors of her hair changing.

No one says anything about the red-orange strands
of her hair fallen to the floor in her hospital room.
Their feet rustle rattlesnakes among the crispy leaves
as they pretend she is still fire and glory.
Having your days numbered is punishment enough.

Soon there is no recourse but to pull the plug.
The ground, stiff with rage, splinters shovels.
Trees grieve and shrink into stick figures.
Bitterness becomes an art form.
Tears hurt so much that even they seep into bone.

IN THE NIGHTCLUB

Winter always waits by the mirrored wall,
smoking one cigarette after another.
Everyone is afraid to look into his strobe-light eyes,
fluttering them into hollow shells of themselves
by the time he's done French kissing them.

But he usually dances alone.
It is then the music stops and everyone stares
when he continues moving to the silence
that only he hears. He shows no embarrassment
when he catches sight of their gapes.

They come here every night for his magic.
You could say that he's developed quite a reputation,
mostly what a terrible husband he would make.
All that is quickly forgotten when they catch
a single tear melting down his porcelain cheek.

WINTER'S EX-GIRLFRIEND

Spring is a girl who's cried all night
only to find that morning easily forgives
the coldness of him having left her
stranded among the thicket of evergreens,
where rabbits dart and deer forage.

With a kiss of sun each day, she will gather up
all her strength, blessing the stiff soil
with the thawing of frozen tears seeping
as she sleeps, and make true her dream of
the day when her fingers are no longer numb.

The one who left her will become a puddle
when she rises to her full height and looks ahead.
Summer, her true love, will soon fall for her,
and she will one day die in his giddy arms.
But *shh*. Don't tell her. She's got a poor heart.

THE MOP-HAIRED BOY

Summer is a mop-haired toothy-grinned boy
who's never had to work a single day in his life.
Lanky yet never gawky, he ambles by
all the girls with petals in their hair
oozing gasps of nectar in his wake.

Full of weed-induced giggles, he lazes about
and says, "Man, what's happening," a lot.
Nights of fireflies puncture the haze of his vision.
He inhales the poppy scents of romance,
but it's not enough. So heroin it is.

He doesn't understand why nobody wants him now.
He's forgotten how one can stink after not bathing so long.
Forced to enter a methadone clinic, he cuts his hair.
Seeing his own pock-marked face in the mirror
for the first time is a terrible autumn.

THE RED MAPLE WIFE

My maple hair has caught fire.
I have been sitting too long in this backyard chair,

fallen asleep from the laziness of days gone by.
My hairdresser never told me she'd leave.

I thought my hair would be fully photosynthesized,
thick and fluffy with sparrows darting in and out,

always alerting everyone to my stately beauty,
but no, I find that I've developed too much chlorophyll.

My kingdom of backyard may seem small,
but my follicles are fierce. I respect no propriety

when I spread underground rumors of my invincibility
across borders. Everyone knows my true age,

a lifetime of rings from remarrying Mr. Spring again.
I know how he's seduced everyone in sight.

Worse yet, he knows just how much loneliness costs me.
He doesn't care to understand how much I've primped

and saved so much of my blood for him. From this chair,
I see him still flirting with pretty young saplings,

whispering promises of marrying them once he divorces
me, this gargantuan bitch with prickly jowls.

I don't understand how he could so easily forget
how these anorexic babes, full of puffy dreams,

never survive the first bitch-slap of snow. They will
wither. He always leaves them once he remembers

what a tough bitch I am when friends abandon him.
I always have a field day in divorce court.

Now homeless, he begs to sleep with me.
I know he'll leave me again, but he's so damn beautiful.

SQUATTERS

Their nests are easily overlooked there in the trees
until the first whip of November brings
your eyes scanning the industrial gray skies.

There, and everywhere, spiky hands hold
the mottled globes woven with twig and leaf.
Their arms are lined with chain-link veins.

Clumps of snow sift through the cracks of cradle
where babies spent childhoods squalling for worms,
rarely wondering why they were up on high.

Every spring the birds return, seeking out
abandoned treefront properties to renovate as their own.
First come, first serve always apply. No counteroffers.

Sometimes they're stuck with real fixer-uppers.
They recycle twigs that no one wants, weaving them
like fingers enmeshed in prayer against rain.

When their children have flown the nest at last,
it is soon time to skip town and head south before
the gangs of winter declare war on them all.

All these homes are rumbled by the whims of violence.
Shingles of clotted leaves sway to the sidewalk.
Neighborhoods go bad up north at this time of year.

PROBATION

Days of white don't seem so pure anymore.
They linger like Scrooge's little fingers
that just won't stop tapping on your shoulder,
reminding you there's still a death sentence.
Your house is a prison of unpaid debts.

Then comes a cardinal hopping about,
its sharp feathers startling like spurts of blood.
Puddles of grass congregate in protest.
Your heart picks up an extra beat, a lilt.

You open the window for a quick waft,
but roars of chill rush in, a pipe organ
echoing in the chapel of last hopes.
Ice-covered leaves sway like lynched bodies.
You're next. Spring hasn't got a single prayer.

DEBUTANTES

Tentativeness coagulates the blood of bulbs.
Too many April rains sparks revolution:

they strip away all their clothes
until their lingerie hang and taunt.

The dull grass blades slake off
the drabness of huddled waiting.

Each blade will prance sharply,
fence with each other for clarity.

They learn to whisper names well
enough to make us go mad,

trampling their bruised egos
until they revolt into a mob of green,

their prickly swords firmer than ever.
Then it's time for a mass crew cut.

In the distance the gowned babes giggle.
Springtime is an endless ball.

THE SABOTEUR

The papier-mâché headquarters leaked
wasps checking in and out
under the eave of our new garage.

I stared up at their pin-striped
business suits, their stings
taut briefcases in case of attack.

I aimed my hoe's weight but missed.
The garage wall shuddered. They never took
notice of this quavering patriot below.

I swung up this time and dented the hole,
bankrupturing coal-dusted kernels
that popped into a swarm of angry clients.

I dropped the hoe and hid next door.
They bumped shoulders into each other
while their paperwork hung exposed.

They consolidated into a single jet,
levitating to some country across the street.
They were still full of secrets for sale.

TWO APPLE TREES

No one knew when they were planted,
but there the two appeared, mysteriously

like buildings having always existed
with no traces of history revealing

a time of undeveloped lots. They stood apart
between a small house and our large house.

The shorter tree stood in our eastern backyard.
She was wide-hipped and long-armed.

Every May her wafting blossoms lifted me,
as if my feet were given tiny wings,

high enough to enable me to inhale
the sweetness around which bees,

strangely fat and dropping out of nowhere,
demanded a cut in the line of my vision.

Her branches bobbed under the weight of bees.
The white petals scattered tears in the wind.

Her branches stretched far south.
My father put a pale blue wooden table

in her shade. Summers her apples thudded, rolled
off the table. Bruises, oozing, buzzed with flies.

The other westerly tree—well, you could say
he was a lanky tall fella, his brim of leaves

tipped so low you could see only his twisted body,
stiff and skeletony. His peppery bark flaked off

like poker chips. The apples from his hat
felt like gambles of dice that only landed

exactly the same way on the thick grass.
He leaned by our three-door garage

as if its roof was his bar counter.
But no drinks could be had.

The stranded cowboy that he was
kept his face long hidden from hers

as the sweetness of tart blood circulated
deep in the veins of their underground love.

Us kids were too busy rounding up
their bitter fruits for Mom's applesauce

to notice how these two trees stayed
steadfast, never looking at each other

through the whiplash of seasons,
but forever aching to inch closer.

DRAGONFLIES

Spin us another thread in the air
where dead mosquitoes knot,
stitching up our nightly quilts,
squared of hunger and hunt,
swinging from the clothesline
between dawn and dusk.

We nymph from egg to adulthood,
blessed with the innate gift to sew.
Four months are all what we've got.
We bustle about, buzzing gossip and tips
as we weave through the cattails.
Life is a constant state fair.

Come September we will die.
It'll be too cold for mosquitoes to flit
like the lazy beer drinkers that they are.
We soon starve our energy to browse.
Fireflies punctuate our funerals.
The swamp is an empty fairground.

Flaps of our wings disintegrate,
ripped pieces of fabric floating
past mallards judging us one more time
before that tarp of snow and ice
submerges our prize-winning handiwork.
Spring thaw is our favorite needle.

MOTHLIGHT

They try to paint on the canvas of night
with their powdery paste of summer light
but nothing, nothing ever looks right.

The bulb glowing under the eave is too bright.
Their wingbrushes splatter dabs of white,
rather like specks across chondrite.

But their perspectives are too skewed tight.
Their sense of composition is a jumbled fright.
They don't know when to stop and exit stage right.

They all want to be Edward Hopper's acolyte.
They never learn his visual tricks, the sleight
of wing required to strike the perfect sight

of sister moon whispering *midnight, midnight,*
rolling afar from love's unseen klieg light.
Suddenly sensing bats nearby, they drop in height.

They return to where their enflamed hearts ignite.
They're still seduced by the mysteries of porchlight.
Trying to make great art is like surviving owl in flight.

CHLOROPHYLL
after S.W.G.

Miles and miles threading through the woods,
I lulled myself into a sleep, not even feeling
the crash of my body into dead pine needles.

As the night blanket crept across my face,
I felt the weight of your boots tiptoeing
across my eyelids flickering, a sparrow's wings.

I felt your shadow pausing, turning, crisscrossing
until I was razored into shreds by your silence.
My bones collapsed, powder off ashen logs.

My veins winded rivulets through layers of leaves
rotting and dank, full of swelter and swarm.
The only thing left intact was the shell of my face.

Your fingertips pressed tentatively, slowly
across my forehead, loosening the clumps,
fists opening up flowers petals springing.

You barely graze the grass of my beard.
I try to whisper. Sun rays drop dew on me
awakening, tendrils rising up to encircle you.

III

TWO NESTS

You knew how to gift in the way Nature didn't care to give.
Each box sent to me was lovingly sealed with transparent tape.
Even the placement of my mailing address was precise
as was your handwriting curlicued with a little flair.
I felt blessed each time I found a present awaiting me.

*

The trails that forked and reforked through pine and birch
up and down against your cliff's edges overlooking Lake Superior
wove and unwove memories of Rocky, his tail perking
happily with his nose vacuuming the air for a feast of scents,
as he darted among the tall grasses leaning on each other.

*

One box of yours brought forth a bough of evergreen branches
clipped—*just so!*—to present a fallen bird's nest. Inside,
the slenderest stalks of grass were molded into a womb.
Tiny curls of birch bark and puffs of fur jeweled its walls.
The nest became a holy relic on the altar of my windowsill.

*

You took the scraps from the upscale restaurant where you worked
and fed them to the scrawny brown foxes awaiting your presence
in the shadow of your house holding strong against the glare
scintillating off the waves of Lake Superior.
The trees spanned a patchy curtain against such brightness.

*

Another box surprised me with a globe-sized nest
with a hole big enough for three bees to pass through.
Its gray paperness screamed fragility. Inside
a tiny chunk of honeycomb was a tossed orphanage.
A dead bumblebee was perched on the hole's edge.

                    *

Rocky always walked carefully to your cliff's edge
where Lake Superior blurred into a hazy horizon.
He instinctively knew this was not a place to run freely.
The splashes lashed below against the rocks.
Hearing the threat of danger was enough.

                    *

As each winter passed through my treeless courtyard,
I bowed my head before my two holy relics of our friendship
on the windowsill. Each time I watered the plants,
the evergreen branches cradling the nests turned more rust
from time and sun, embrittled into broken promises.

                    *

How was I to know that the gray nest once belonged to hornets?
Had Nature lied to me, like yellowjackets masquerading as bees?
Why hadn't anyone warned me that Rocky would turn deaf,
blind, and arthritic with a dash of dementia? Why
hadn't anyone warned me that even you would ghost me?

                    *

Once opened, your boxes overflowered with tenderness,
never with dainties, but with stiff stems outfitted
with circular pieces of paper ruffled into petalled crowns.
They still huddle together under the dust of years in their corner.
I haven't the heart to shake them free of you.

                    *

The saplings that you'd planted a long time ago whisper
in a language that only mushrooms can translate.
Trees hold steady in a way that our friendship hasn't.
Rocky is dead. The stability of seasons is out of whack.
My heart is a fallen nest. It is empty without you.

                                                    CHLOROPHYLL

MY DRACAENA DAUGHTERS

1.

You three were regal and prickly in purplish greens,
beautiful small maidens with bowed heads, on sale for $10.
I couldn't resist. You stayed together in the same pot,

huddling together that summer, always glancing back at me.
I tried to cajole you three with the wine of water
and the joyful music of sun coming from the south.

You three still kept your faces turned away, noses up
in the air, as you fanned yourselves with murmurs.
Then the frost of winterlight coated your view outside.

An abandoned shovel slept on the snow-covered courtyard.

2.

I moved you three to the windowsill in my bedroom.
The temperature of loneliness dropped below zero.
Banished, you shook the dust off your shoulders.

Your bitterness melted in my caresses when I watered.
You three swallowed pride as you rose twice the height
of when I first saw you, my fountain princesses.

Your fingers wove together a hint of fire and chlorophyll,
pushing aside yellowing threads of gossip and lies,
in this loom of my bedroom secrets where I ached.

You three speculated about the empty space on my bed.

3.

You are the bosom buddies I never had. May you teach me
the art of stitching glances together to tell a story
I've yet to learn, the dense fool that I am, how to get right.

May you three give me quiet looks of *harumph*
when I try to fill the empty space with someone else
obviously wrong. May your leafy fingers foretell my fortunes,

and warn. May you three allow me entanglement deep
in your roots where I've poured a pitcher of tears.
Please let me be your protector of sun and water.

I am your father. Everything else's negotiable.

THE COMPOST PILE

Even though autumn's long gone, I hand you a rake.
Seasons have turned everything into a leafy muck.

Spread the ice salt across the cheeks of my face.
The indentations will irrigate my frozen tears.

Come spring, these crystals will tadpole away
in the melted rivers mashed from slush.

Arms of grass will stretch and rise from their beds.
It will feel so good to sip water and sunshine again.

Bees will swap pollen from one flower to another,
stealing precious nectar right under everyone's noses.

But summer alone could never cleanse my acne scars of you.
Looks like I'll have to bury you all over again.

THE TULIP DIVA

On an incline overrun with dandelions,
she stands tall, its piercing red petals
upturned to reveal mascara-laced eyes,
spitting *bon mots* of butter and fire
at everyone strolling by on the sidewalk.
The sun is her spotlight.
No one understands how much bitterness
was required, a lonely winter
under a thick and mottled blanket
frozen over her head, to split
open her heart's bulb up to the skies,
pushing past the spring torrents,
a plea for a tenderness of touch
just as her eyes narrow
at the soldier bees hovering just so,
scraping the last of her sweetness
off her pollen-swollen tongue
in front of everyone. Oh, the humiliation!
Mere weeks later, she stoops alone
amidst a puddle of dull red chips
in a sea of wizened whiskers.
Her waxy rags will be sliced at last
in the lawnmower's war march,
but the undying romantic in her
prays for a return to the stage. This time,
in the dreamless sleep of winter,
she promises to deny herself the pleasure
of lashing out and allow herself the agony
of offering herself up for a bouquet.

MADEMOISELLE ROSE

Death is the quickest path to love.
This is how I will know where he's gone:

the soil underneath is rich with blood.
Its brown is so dark; almost crimson.

Drops of dew are the tears I shed;
only that no one knows it's come from me.

I was betrothed until that bitch wind
tumbled into the ballroom of summer,

shaking me of all my confidence.
Was I not radiant enough, with a glow?

I wove my heart into my hairdo,
layered and frosted shimmeringly red.

Bees fussed over me, but they stole my nectar,
the love juice I'd saved for my man.

No one knows where he's gone. Onstage,
I'm a torch song caught in repose.

Oooh over my perfume if you must;
refocus your camera lens if you like,

but don't come too close. Stop. Right there is fine.
I don't care anymore how I look.

My leaves are fists wound up. Too much waiting.
The thorns on my anorexic stem deaden.

You may kiss me, but only once. My lips, chapped
with cuts, crumble, unheard on the wind.

FITTONIAS

1.

Centuries ago, the Incas walked
among us fittonias in the rainforest.

We stayed neutral in their fatal war
between Huascar and Atahualpa,

brothers fighting to control Cuzco.
Then the pasty-faced Francisco Pizarro

showed up and conquered everything
else until these brothers fell. We wept

so much that our green leaves tattooed
the skeletons of our permanent tears.

2.

Centuries later, my kidnapped ancestors
were put on cranky buses in all directions.

They were spout-fed the water of lies
of how they'd return home to Peru.

They would reunite with our true caretakers
cooing in the language of Quechua.

I myself have traveled a long way
to America. I'm a prisoner of war.

I have no other story. I miss my past.
Mist me again. I've forgotten how to cry.

LAKEWOOD CEMETERY
for S.W.G.

The man I could've been had you loved me
lies buried mute, unmarked among tombstones.

His blue eyes once lit up like daffodils,
startling whispers of the spring to come.

I have flowers but no vase to place them
next to this freshly potted rectangle.

My body, not quite emptied of you, roots
in embraces gnarly-brittle as bones.

Soil sludges through my veins until I worm
close to the ghost reduced to nights alone.

I tell him that he was not wrong to love you.
He grunts, turns over, and goes back to sleep.

The atlas of your uncashed affections
creeps wrinkly rivers all over his back.

The flickers of regret tickle his eyelids.
A stranded cicada scuttles away.

MEDUSA'S HAIR

Her strands of thyme snarl
toward the sun. Each time
I rotate her on the sill, tongues
of tendril menace me,
then weave and hiss love songs
to the sun who shrugs.

She recoils when I caress
her springy afro, never seeing
her face. Legend had it
that anyone seeing her eyes
would turn to stone. Her shoulders
slump when I tear at her mane.

She threatens curses with averted eyes.
My kitchen is a far call from home.
Her strands, once aloft in my hands,
twist, turn in the sizzle of oil.
She is all spit. I get stoned
inhaling her musk off my fingers.

THE FIRST MUSK

The warm air, thick
with misted humidity,
hung low around us
one February morning.
I dawdled behind
my deaf classmates,
ski hats and mittens
stashed into our jackets
left unzipped
in the hot steam
of the crisp sun
magnified through
the glass high above us
where the crystal lace
of ice and snow
graced the edges
of each pane.
Facing the seven of us
(including a teacher
and her aide)
crowding the aisles
between tables
loaded with plants
of all kinds and sizes
in green plastic pots
labeled with numbers
stood a tall woman
who smiled a lot,
who wore long frizzy hair,
who wore jeans
with wet knee stains.
I was surprised
this hadn't bothered her.
Mom always used
a dark lime-green
polyurethane knee pad
on the kitchen floor

when she washed it
clean of footprints
every Friday afternoon.
Why couldn't this woman
do the same thing?
Standing before us,
she explained
slowly and carefully,
as if she was afraid
to shout at us,
forbidden to sign
and too young then
to question such fallacy,
how a plant could grow
from a seed
*Look at how small
this is* into *This!*:
a tall plant in a huge pot.
It didn't look
like anything familiar,
not from the summers
I'd spent across the street
from my house
in the woods
where breezes sifted
dandelion whiskers
flurrying through
the saplings
crowding against
each other, spectators
lining the motorcycle trails
us kids raced on foot
in search of
another adventure.
Foxes and rabbits
startled us
with their tails,

tipped with white,
hopping back
into the basket
of tall grasses
that itched our faces
when we plowed
forward north,
off the trails,
where the cave-ins,
remnants of iron mines,
its steel shafts
long dismantled,
already blanketed
with the grass of time
sloping down
to a circus of saplings.
Down there we explored,
darting around the slender
trees, not knowing that
a few summers from then
a bulge of water would
push up from nowhere,
filling the big holes
and drowning the saplings.
Melted snow would add
to its unmarked depths.
Every winter since
we would be told *Never
go down there!
Too dangerous.
There's no telling how
thin that ice is.*
In the greenhouse
we deaf kids stood,
looking agape
when the woman pushed
her long fingers
right into the soil
near the plant's stem
and burrowed
deeper, deeper

Wait I got it
and twisted
her hand just so
until she pulled out
a tiny brown ball,
the smallest potato
I had ever seen.
Every winter
in the evening
my father plotted
on scrap paper
our two gardens
in our backyards
(he'd owned two houses,
ours and the one next door
that he rented out,
and a third lot
for our three-car garage),
poring through
Burpee Seed catalogs
while the nine of us kids
ran around the house,
all cooped up
while he awaited
the prison of winter
to release all of us
in the freedom of summer.
He rotated the crops
between our two gardens
so the rows every year
were never the same.
He made us siblings
march up and down
the foot trails so
they wouldn't feel mushy
between the ridges
where he'd planted
one seed after another
and anointed each seed
with a pour of water.
We had to stamp hard

until we felt hardness,
a sense of something
like crooked concrete.
Then the rains came.
The seeds sprouted.
One row had fuzzy
carrot tops that drooped.
Another row exploded
in upturned lettuce wigs.
A short row shrouded
budding watermelons
in huge talon leaves,
nestled in springy tendrils.
Two rows lined crooked
daggers until they turned
into swords of corn.
The sugar snap peas
were my favorite snack.
I stole a few pods
whenever I was hungry.
Mom always complained
there were never enough.
She gave us kids dirty looks.
Mornings each of us took
turns to pluck out weeds,
those errant fingers
peeking out of the soil.
Done, we came running
back into the house,
its side door banging
behind us, shouting, *Mom,
I did two rows,
Can I go play now?*
Our fingernails
showed gray crescents
so we enjoyed
clipping our nails
over the opened toilet
where we brushed
away the tiny soil wedges
and made our nails clean.

That was always fun.
The soil we packed
in our two gardens
was only the color
of light brown sugar.
No distinct smell to it.
In the greenhouse
I couldn't stop
staring at the soil's dark
chocolate color.
How could it look so *black*?
The dirt across the street
where mottles of birches
and tall grasses swayed
revealed a rust color,
a nod to the old days
when miners from Croatia,
Finland, Ireland,
Germany, and Poland
slid down into
the gaping shafts,
gods in full mastery
of house-sized machines,
and carve out
huge chunks of iron ore
that would be soon
hauled away by train.
Such glory days
were long gone
by the time I was born.
I didn't understand
how these immigrant men,
inured to long hours
in the pits of earth,
were already longing
for something real, perhaps
a song from their childhoods
back in the Old World
that would root them firmly
home here in America.
In the greenhouse

I looked up at the woman.
I don't recall what I asked,
but she answered,
her eyes alight,
handing me the baby potato,
more like a marble
really, the kind
the hearing boys and I
won on the ground
outside Ripley School
where we twisted
the heel edges of our tenners,
into the hard dirt until
the hole was big enough
to accommodate
the many scores
of marbles we flicked
with our thumbs
as far as we could
during recess each fall.
We traded marbles
every single day.
It meant we were boys,
a world of our own.
I didn't quite understand
how the hearing world worked,
but I knew it involved
strong and nimble thumbs.
I didn't know it then
but those days
when I finally felt a part
of the world around me
were coming to a close.
Soon the marbles
would disappear
into our pockets,
as if they'd become
objects of shame,
and give way
to standing around
nonchalantly

by the vacated holes,
making lots of talk
about the TV shows
we'd seen the night
before, sometimes
reenacting them
but nothing like how
all of us had moved
in slow motion,
wanting to be the next
six-million-dollar man.
We would all be Steve Austin.
Their mouths now moved
quickly with new words
I'd never lipread before,
and I wanted to know
when we could play marbles
again. I felt a slight rage
rise, just like how Jack
had grown his magic beanstalk,
from the handful
of marbles I'd caressed
in the secrecy of my pocket.
I'd worked so hard
to win each single one,
some truly beautiful;
I even practiced
secretly after school!
And all for what?
I didn't grasp yet
the stir of hormones
lurking beneath
our skins, waiting to shed
the smoothness
for a coat of peach fur,
or that in a few years
our voices would crack
into a deeper register.
Without warning
they turned to me.
I was that waif-boy

with those things
in his ears. Nope,
I wasn't one of them.
On the bus home
that afternoon, I sat
near the front,
no longer cool enough
to sit near the hearing boys
in the back seats,
and felt the coolness
of my marbles
clinking softly
between my fingers
as I watched the boys
jab each other
in the armpit
and break into guffaws
in the panoramic mirror
hovering above
the driver's bald pate.
The next morning
I saw how they moved
off to the side. I joined
my deaf classmates.
It was the first time
I came to understand
deaf kids weren't cool.
In the greenhouse
I weighed the baby potato
like a marble. So light,
unimaginably so.
They weren't the potatoes
my mother peeled
every Sunday noon
before boiling them
for mashing. I looked
at the baby potato
cradled in my hand.
Its dark residue of soil
had been wiped away.
I looked up at her.

She probably asked,
What's wrong?
I walked over to the big pot
and touched the soil.
It was loose. Soft.
Not densely packed.
I scooped a little bit.
Inhaling it, I felt a shock.
The smell on my fingers
was sublime, unlike anything
I'd experienced. Primal,
it sang of something
deeper than the earth itself,
its purest essence.
It flashed me back
to lazy July afternoons
where I spread
a rug on the grass
under a canopy of shade
and fell asleep
while cracks of sun
crisscrossed my face.
Awakening an hour later
was my favorite part.
My head woozy,
full of dreams elsewhere,
I always forgot
where I was
for a moment
as the sun lapped my face
like a happy dog.
I wanted to believe
I was transported
to another world.
What country would I find
if I didn't recall
which way was home?
In the greenhouse,
staring at my fingers,
I didn't know soil
could smell like *that*,

so rich and heavenly.
It was the first musk
that made sense to me,
my first flowering
into the world of men,
secreted by pheromones.
I wanted to rub my face
across my hands.
Suddenly I didn't
need marbles anymore.
These days
I roast baby potatoes
until perfectly marbled
from a thin patina
of olive oil
in a cast iron skillet.
Eating these
brings me back
to the boy
who nearly became
a man too soon.

THE CUTTING
for J.O.

He was my stalk, and I his branch.
He protected me from the birds
that swooped down, hoping for an overlooked berry
hanging from my arm.

Instead I was deemed too large.
Lopped off, I sulked in a glass of water on the sill,
my roots whitened raw with tears.
The sun filtered in my water was pure morphine.

I grew gnarly nails from hunger and madness.
Finally allowed into soil, I mined
rich ores of minerals and nutrients. I swore
never to let go. My muscular roots thickened.

As I turned all my eyelids upward to the sun,
I felt a tender itch sprout off my side.
I cradled him until he was ready to go off on a limb.
One day, my boy, they'll take you away from me.

LILACS

My father had always hated them.
Its sickly sweet smell was an assault,

a virus worse than invasions of
thick dandelion whiskers parachuting.

Two lilac bushes loitered proudly
in front of Mrs. Lewinski's house

two doors away on Oak Street. Each spring
I always stopped to inhale a fresh needle,

laden with that mix of pollen and nectar,
into the crook of my nose, my veins

throbbing at the slightest twitch.
These lilacs in bloom were pure crack.

Thirty-three years ago my father died.
I still shoot up my nose when I see them

lined with feather boas of blossoms
trembling from bees policing the pollen.

I wish he were still alive to lament
how this neighborhood was going to seed.

THIS NAMELESS FIELD

Among the strident goldenrods,
we kids knew exactly where to find
clusters of barely pink strawberries
and avoid the thorny roses,
abandoned when the owner arrived
to find his old house burning
one spring afternoon.

We watched the firefighters from our porch.
The owner didn't rebuild. He left,
the winds brushing the ashes away,
tumbling across roof shingles
spun about like frisbees. They became
patches waiting to be sown
right onto the unkempt quilt

of grass and goldenrod. We dared
not approach the charred remains,
just like the cave-ins that hadn't then
swollen with water. They were mammoth
holes sloped with young trees
trying to stand upright. We didn't
understand how this nameless field

could be hived with ghosts invisible,
their memories of the Old World
still fresh with ache in their bones,
their exhilaration of pulleying
carts of iron ore up from the pits,
their horror when a tunnel buckled under.
Sometimes nothing more

could be done after extricating
the dead from the rubble
and tearing down the headframe.
Yet the more they dug nearby, the more
Ironwood would get emptied and buried

in their glory days of war overseas.
We were all Americans, weren't we?

Nearby a thin row of birch saplings stood.
We didn't know how quickly
they'd grow tall into a muscular wall
that would've blocked our view
of St. Michael's spire had it
not been razed for a parking lot.
Who knew our church would fall too?

Then came another summer when we came
unexpectedly across those roof shingles,
having already forgotten the burnt house,
the man who'd owned it, and the roses too.
We lifted each tar-hot shingle to find
tiny snakes electric-shocked by the sun
writing across the white-yellow grass.

We gathered up their squiggly forms
in our hands. We squealed at them
trying to wrestle free of us. We giggled
at their desperation, not knowing
that souls, like ours, bound to this field would
be forever excavated under our footprints.
We didn't know we'd become caretakers.

A MOST MYSTERIOUS GARDENER
for L.B.

What you are to me, I don't understand:
why me? You have unfurled vines of tendrils
from the canopied trellis of my soul.
I thought I was tough enough to withstand
the weight of dark grapes waiting to be plucked
and pulverized into such sweet red wine.
I thought I'd been doomed to tart bitterness.

My first summer of you has decomposed
old roots steaming hurt in my compost pile.
You noticed not whether my grapes were ripe
but how shakily I had held my ground.
Unasked, you righted me and pruned dead leaves
from my face. You radiated water.
Oh, how I laughed! My heart blossomed wine.

IV

STUMPS

We hated each other in the beginning.
We all did. We silently plotted.
Our souls were tight fists of seed.
No air inside. No sun.
No one talked to each other.
The eyes of our souls stayed upward.
Our damn parents kept blocking the sun.

Dead leaves sheathed us.
The blanket of white death weighed us down.
We began to hear the faintest hum.
What was it? Why did it sound strangely familiar?
But none of us dared ask each other.
The unclear sound drilled deep into our dreams.
We awoke to the nightmare of eerie pitch.

Our bodies split apart.
We didn't know it then but puberty had set in.
Full of hormones, we pushed upward.
No more cold, no more wet.
The sun would welcome us. It had to!
Childhood memories of its warmth had sustained us.
We found our fingernails turning green.

Our bodies, limber that spring, lengthened.
Didn't matter that there wasn't enough sun.
The brashness of our youth was on our side.
We still ignored each other.
We were still flexing our muscles.
We knew only a few of us could survive.
There was only enough soil to go around.

By summer's end, a few of our siblings had died.
We didn't stop to mourn.
We were too consumed with nightmares.
We didn't understand the seasons.
Why those dead leaves? Again? What for?

We worried about the sun slipping away.
The chill gnawed at our translucent skins.

We shivered in all that dark.
We were still not talking to each other.
We constantly compared among ourselves.
Finally the warm light elongated over shadow.
Our stiff toes wriggled at last.
We noted those who hadn't survived the relentless cold.
We were secretly happy. More sun for us!

Oh, how we grew that summer! Just shimmery.
We felt proud of the way our leaves unfurled.
We felt our legs, feet, toes dig deeper.
Who knew there could be so much warmth down there?
That a few more of us died was no huge loss.
We looked up at our parents.
Their silence still unnerved us.

We wanted to ask them questions.
But they still blocked the sun.
How we hated them, resented them.
Why couldn't they just drop their arms?
It was the least they should do for us.
We began to learn names for everything.
Sun: winter, spring, summer, fall.

The rhythm of seasons comforted us.
Our beings thickened and deepened.
An occasional thunderstorm would split one of us.
We felt the first rip of mortality strike deep.
We averted our eyes when humans arrived with chainsaws.
We felt speechless at the sight of those stumps.
Surely we'd amounted to more than that!

Then came the day when our parents were felled.
Our hearts lurched when humans yelled, "Timber!"
The sound of chainsaws rattled our dreams.
Didn't matter that the sun was completely ours.
Torrential rains soaked our beings.
Unfettered, we reached upward to the heavens.
We felt woozy-hearted from the challenge.

Humans never saw what we were doing beneath the surface.
Our legs, multiplying, crisscrossed like trapeze artists.
Soon we found ourselves touching each other.
We jolted back from the unexpected intimacy.
We began to talk about our parents.
The memories of our first summer made us cry.
We found ourselves stretching and weaving legs, feet, toes.

Feeling secure, we turned again to the sun.
We felt the long-forgotten hum resound.
Our stump ancestors, given up for dead, were still alive.
They were singing the story of generations past.
We learned the mystery of seasons.
We stitched further back in time's tapestry.
We bled our sweaty sugar into the arms of our ancestors.

Seasons came and went. We barely noticed.
We were too busy telling each other stories.
We oohed and ahhed over the tiny babies in our hands.
Then suddenly we had to learn how to parent.
It was the worst lesson of our lives. We were inconsolable.
How could we shake them off? Just wasn't done.
We felt less guilty after each storm. It wasn't our fault.

The ghosts of our parents whispered in our veins.
The only way to survive this was to ignore our own babies.
No! We wanted to have them back in our arms.
That first winter we said nothing to each other.
We wove our unseen bodies for family's warmth.
Our dreams, commingling, lost track of whose belonged to whom.
Only through loss will our stories never decompose.

NOVEMBER ROOTS

The tree that once towered above
my landlord's garage has been chopped down,
gone, bedded
with dead leaves raked
over to hide the earth's pockmark.
The stump is twisted to the side.

These fingers, once proud, weaken.
They let go handfuls of soil,
losing spine of trunk at last
in the vast pockets of earth.
There's nothing left to forgive.
It is my turn now to age.

FIREWOOD

1.

At thirteen, my body was
a sapling, nearly rootless.
My arms and legs shivered
easily in September.
The winds constantly uprooted me.
I had to seek firmer ground.

2.

A pale-eyed man with a Stormy Kromer cap
grunted as he used his feet to push
the last of the two cords of firewood
out from the back of his truck.
The wood was strewn like popcorn
everywhere in our backyard.

3.

Days my father stood behind the meat counter
at Lopez's IGA off U.S. 2. He wore a white cap.
His apron was occasionally marked by blood.
He was full of smiles. His wallet was thick
with pictures of all nine of us. Customers rolled
their eyes each time he had to show a new picture.

4.

Hardened by the seasons,
the firewood twisted and gnarled
each time I held out my arms,
a cradle sheathed in sweatshirt.
I nearly buckled from its weight of
rage from having been chopped down.

5.

The gap into the basement measured
only one foot high and two feet wide.
We siblings turned into an assembly line,
stacking wood in my arms, passing
each piece through the gap, stacking it again
in a cold corner next to my father's office.

6.

In the basement blackened by winter,
my father sat by the furnace,
his shoulders lit by a lone bulb,
as he read his cheap westerns.
I never understood why he needed to be alone.
Hadn't he been bragging about us?

7.

At sixteen, I found myself in the arms
of a handsome tree. I trembled,
intoxicated by the power of seasons
inherent in his seed. What was happening?
He said that I'd need to leave this town
one day. The fact weighted my feet.

8.

We siblings rarely ventured downstairs in winter.
The chill felt ready to pounce on our bones.
The great wall of firewood, across from the stairs,
was a monster, its innards filled with bugs.
Only our parents refilled the furnace and stoked it.
The heat seeped upstairs in our house.

9.

My father is dead. I've long since moved away.
The furnace still works at my mother's house.
She now hires someone to stack the wood.
The basement is a skeleton of its former self.
I stoke the words of what should've been said
in the furnace of memory. My book comes up empty.

THE BIRCH TREE

A lifetime ago when I'd never thought
in terms of decades passing,
my father planted a small birch sapling
on the southwest border between our house
and the house we rented out next door.

Growing up, it's seen us nine children
chase the winds in the backyard and move away.
Each time we visit, we're always surprised
by how tall, even angrily, it overlooks
my mother's creaky swinging bench.

A makeshift shack, made of discarded lumber
and siding, used to sit right over there,
but it was torn down after one summer.
The other shack was enough.
That too was eventually torn down.

It has also watched our family dog die
of a heat stroke in the sun.
Then the vegetable gardens were carpeted
with grass. The dirt basketball court
disappeared with the dog house too.

The gnarly apple tree that lent shade
to our lanky picnic table was cut down.
The clothesline stretched between the two T's
is the only thing left. Even now it's hanging
onto freshly washed clothes waving bye-bye.

After so many summers of betrayal
and abandonment, it knows that one day
it will get chopped down like so many others.
But not now. Oh, not now, not ever,
not while I still have a lifetime left to go.

LICHEN

Those gray crumbly fingers reaching still
for something like love but not quite
against the tree's jittery frostbites
and snowy epaulets. No, they won't be stilled!

There is the tree, and there is flight:
they caress the intimacy of bark chilled,
those gray crumbly fingers reaching still
for something like love but not quite.

The late April sun has begun to spill
down buckets of warmth, shadowing heights
they must scale toward twilight.
Only the most secret afternoons can heal

those gray crumbly fingers reaching still
for something like first love, but not quite.

WHITE PINES

1.

A long time ago young men wishing to be tall
scaled the mast of my octopus arms
and scanned the horizon of Lake Superior
for a glimmer of Canada. Usually we were cut down.

2.

The long prickly fur that covers my arms
shields the damp ground from the sun.
My deepened feet wade lazily in the tidal soil.
Worms sniggling around my toes itch right.

3.

The world of men down there has its own rules.
They don't realize how us pines must band together,
weaving arms out of loneliness against the skies.
We are bred to do without women, yet we ache.

4.

Squirrels, birds, and deer know I've fathered
these woods cascading like ocean waves
up and down the Porcupine Mountains.
They know safety is complete in my shadow.

5.

Men are always angry at how I could dominate.
My one stem is always thick and erect,
always dribbling with resin even in cold rains.
Years only strengthen my veins unlike theirs.

6.

Us pines don't say much. Just listening
to each other breathe is almost too close to sex.
I've never had a woman, but each cone dropped
is a tear for the one I never had. May each breed.

7.

Every generation us pines will catch fire.
Stripped to the color of ash, we stand barren.
In the powdery soil are some of our buried cones,
laced with seeds that will split and remember.

8.

Divide me among an ocean of short men
made tall with the affliction of seafaring.
My absence will bequeath to children
the first kiss of sun, the first drench of rain.

THE WOODCARVER

As he slowly guides the chunk of linden
wood inside the lathe of his hands
with slashes of knife,
a misshapen orb slowly becoming
the body of a sparrow puffed up
against the winter to come,
all idle thoughts go:

                  his boy's face.
That beak needs to be smoothed out.
There. Another marriage gone south. Hmm.
That wing is too thick. Just a tiny whit.
Guess it's just me and a little nip.

With his finished bird cradled in hand,
he stands for a moment on the sidewalk,
surrounded by chips curling up
for affection around his feet.

THE PROPERTY LINE

My friend walks me around his ten acres,
pointing out the pine saplings that have died
and the spruce fledglings that should survive.

Each spring he checks the wood stakes marking
the ones he'd planted the year before.
Each stake is a just-in-case tombstone.

He tells me how tall and how long each tree will grow,
and shows me the stump of a red pine that a driver knocked
over from driving off the U.S. 45. Value? $800!

I survey each tall tree and ask him how much
each tree could be worth in an accident. The higher
a tree is, the higher his estimates rise into thousands.

He notices a few saplings he'd accidentally planted
just over the property line. I glance around and ask
if neighbors would chop them down. "Not yet." He shrugs.

These trees, when tall and strong, will defend his honor.
They will bear shining armors of green and bark in battle.
It will take generations to root them out completely.

TREE ON TAYLOR STREET

Once overlooking
Curley's garden,
it had stood
amazingly tall
and brusque
like a celery stick
plopped right
next to a small house
and an unpaved driveway
for so long
that, after having
been away for years,
I had to blink twice
to believe
I wasn't seeing
a ghost tree there
standing not so small
in its place.

SUMMERS AGO ON THIS CORNER
A TANGLE OF PINES

Summers ago on this corner a tangle of pines, all planted closely together at the same time, seemed like a gnarly box, height and width and depth all of equal length, its twiggy threads sticking out and shielding the dark green boughs in a veil of dull gray. The pines weren't fenced in, but their volume of silences all day long kept my youngest sister and me from entering. The fear of being scratched by all those barren branch-claws while weaving up and down among the white-brown pine needles softening our footsteps was too great.

Across the pothole-riven boulevard stood an orange-painted swing set and a seesaw in the middle of another square lot. The two swings hung on a thick pipe, already seasoned with rust; its two pipe-poles were dipped in concrete. Tufts of grass clenched its bases in a vise. Someone always made a point of flinging a swing so hard it would spin and spin until its chains would twist atop the bar. No one could reach the swing. Yet no one ever questioned how those swings were mysteriously brought back to earth. We never pondered if someone from the city had brought a ladder and unwound these swings after mowing the grass, but there they were, awaiting once again the push of our bird's flight of fantasy into the sky above our tenners.

At dusk, owls the color of bark fluttered out of the pines. Bats streaked black lightnings against the darkening canvas of sky. The mosquitoes that had tortured us all day long evaporated into the cool air. Some nights when we felt tired, we lay down on the scratchy grass and looked up. The streetlamp on the corner was dim enough to enable one layer of stars after another to reveal slowly, then quickly, to our naked eyes. None of us knew astronomy, but we didn't need to. Seeing so many stars all at once was enough. No binoculars needed. We hated it when a truck suddenly came out of nowhere, its twin lights slashing across the periphery of our vision, nearly hurting our eyes, and while it disappeared, we had to rest our eyes a second before we could zero back into the infinity unfolding above us. We thought of nothing but how cool it was to see so many stars.

The chill of night shuddered across our skin. We reluctantly pushed ourselves to our feet. When we ambled east on West Oak Street, we stayed quiet. We left behind shadows each time we walked under a streetlamp. We nodded at the houses we passed; we knew all of our neighbors who lived in them. A flicker of television occasionally leaked from their windows. We weren't filled with deep thoughts about the universe. We were thinking of how we needed to be inside our house where our beds awaited us upstairs. There we slept, never knowing that in the hurry of our growing up, we would ache to dream again of pines and owls and swings and stars so clear it'd make us cry, our middle-aged selves wondering whether we had been chasing the wrong mysteries the entire time.

MOTHER BIRCH

What she longed to say
was curled
in the paper of her fist:

such knife-edged
documentation.

*

Each smack of season
fleshed out her skeleton
in fits of hard-earned hope.

The sun and the rain
make the best sisters.

*

She never learned
proper penmanship,
but her blood was ink.

Roots everywhere
bleed stories.

*

In the throttle of forest,
she nevertheless craved
pageantries of green.

Each leaf along her arms
rustles a sequin.

*

Her language is so old
that pages of its dictionary
have scattered among dreams:

how to retrieve them all,
how to translate a single word.

        *

There in her fist, white-
knuckled against scabs of death,
are palimpsests,

stories rewilding like weeds,
rewriting her losses.

ON THE CORNER OF OAK AND SPRUCE
for David Cummer (1956-2022)

On the corner of Oak and Spruce
once stood a magnificent oak tree.
Come autumn it was not shy with its acorns
that then took refuge, furrowing deep
like stones among the grass blades.

Many summers ago I ran barefoot.
The cool green carpet soothed me like lotion
after each tiptoe across a stripe
of baked tar, a band-aid
just melted in a crumbly fissure.

The oak tree has been chopped down
a long time ago. Potholes have proliferated
worse than acorns. Even Norrie School's gone.
There are more FOR SALE signs than neighbors.
My mother is in her 90s already.

The patches across the street where I'd plucked
strawberries have vanished. The prickly roses too.
The thick trees near the cracked cement floor
have given way to a cavalcade of birch in the distance.
It's not the country of my childhood anymore.

Not as many streetlights there stay awake as I do,
and when I do, I catch the silhouette of you
standing tall in the canopy of constellations.
You are an oak tree. I await the fall of your acorns
into my arms, soil enriched with memory.

SAMARA

Our names don't matter.
    The veins of sugar
        from our mapled mother

have pumped into each of us
    a pair of hard-shelled hearts
        containing gonad vials

of blood, of milk,
    of antiquities that tell
        stories on repeat:

the great droughts,
    the seemingly endless feasts
        of mineral and sun, starting

from the first splinter
    of seed so long ago
        we've forgotten their names.

If we name anything,
    it's fiction. It doesn't matter
        anyway. Our wings are spinning.

It is the sweetest vertigo.
    Letting go is a parachute's delight.
        No one had ever warned us.

Disembarked with breezy kiss-offs,
    thousands of us nobodies
        will fight each season to take root,

entangling and disentangling
    a tapestry of history woven underneath
        worms, mushrooms, and moss.

ACKNOWLEDGMENTS

The following poems have appeared in these journals and anthologies:

ArLiJo: "Lichen" and "Off the Cliffs of Lake Superior."
Among the Leaves: Queer Male Poets on the Midwestern Experience (Raymond Luczak, ed., Squares & Rebels): "The Birch Tree" and "On the Corner of Oak and Spruce."
Assaracus: "Chlorophyll," "The Cutting," "Gichigami," "Immigrants," "Mademoiselle Rose," "The Mop-Haired Boy," "The Red Maple Wife," and "White Pines."
BlazeVOX: "The Orange-Haired Girl."
Chaffin Journal: "Two Apple Trees."
Floating Bridge Review: "The Tulip Diva."
Ginosko Literary Journal: "Mothlight."
Halcyon Days: "Fog Off Little Girl's Point."
Heneni Magazine: "Basalt."
It's About Time: A Main Street Rag Anthology (Kathie Giorgio, ed.; Mint Hill Books): "Squatters."
The New Engagement: "Amygdaloid."
Nine Mile: "Stumps" and "Summers Ago on This Corner a Tangle of Pines."
Origins Journal: "My Dracaena Daughters."
Peacock Journal: "Why Giants Don't Exist in the Upper Peninsula."
peculiar journal: "Samara."
Q Review: "In the Nightclub."
Queer Voices of Minnesota: An Anthology (Andrea Jenkins, John Medeiros, and Lisa Marie Brimmer, eds.; Minnesota History Press): "The First Musk."
Rabbit: "Firewood."
RFD: "A Most Mysterious Gardener."
Slipstream: "A Ghost, Halfway There."
SOFTBLOW: "Jaspilites."
Southwest Journal: "Winter's Ex-Girlfriend."
Sweater Weather: "Fittonias," "Medusa's Hair," and "The Saboteur."
Saint Paul Almanac: "The Woodcarver" (originally titled "The Woodcarver on West Seventh Street").
Tiger Moth Review: "The Property Line."
Tiny Seed Literary Journal: "Tree on Taylor Street."

Total Eclipse: "Debutantes."

The Tribe Journal: "The Compost Pile."

The U.P. Reader #2 (Mikel Classen and Deborah K. Frontiera, eds.; Modern History Press): "How Copper Came to the Keweenaw Peninsula."

Walloon Writers Review: "The Birth of Agates" and "Dragonflies."

The Way North: Collected Upper Peninsula New Works (Ron Riekki, ed., Wayne State University Press): "Ontonagon."

Word Fountain: "On Docks Off Eagle Harbor" and "Probation."

Wordgathering: "November Roots."

The following poems were nominated for the Pushcart Prize: "The Mop-Haired Boy" (2011), "Ontonagon" (2013), and "Amygdaloid" (2016).

The author would also like to thank the following folks who've helped with this book in ways large and small over the years: Bryan Borland, John Lee Clark, David Cummer (*in memoriam*), Eric Norris, Tony Santos, and Tom Steele. Many thanks to Stephanie Heit, Mike James, Su Smallen Love, Emily Van Kley, William Reichard, and Pia Taavila-Borsheim for their kind words, and to Shawn Malone for the use of her incredible photograph. And it's always a joy to find Victor R. Volkman waiting at the finish line!

CHLOROPHYLL

ABOUT THE AUTHOR

Raymond Luczak grew up in Ironwood and Houghton in Michigan's Upper Peninsula. He is the author and editor of many books, including the U.P.-related titles *Compassion, Michigan: The Ironwood Stories* (Modern History Press) and *This Way to the Acorns: Poems* (Handtype Press). His book *once upon a twin: poems* (Gallaudet University Press) was selected as a U.P. Notable Book for 2021. His work has appeared in *Poetry*, *Prairie Schooner*, and elsewhere. An inaugural Zoeglossia Fellow, he lives in Minneapolis, Minnesota. He can be found online at raymondluczak.com.